Brandon
the
BEE™

Fulton Books, Inc.
Meadville, PA

Published by Fulton Books 2020

ISBN 978-1-64654-233-8 (hardcover)
ISBN 978-1-64654-232-1 (digital)

Printed in the United States of America

Brandon the BEE™

Bee Kind

Jan Sherman

All my life, I've lived in a beehive near hedges. Flowers have nectar, which is my favorite food. It gives me the energy to buzz around the neighborhood and bee kind to all my friends.

Today everything changed. *Thwack!* *Thwack!* *Kerplunk*! The hedges flopped to the ground.

All my flowers with yummy nectar were gone!
How could this bee! What was I going to eat?

4

I needed to get piles and piles of sweet nectar in my belly before I lost all my energy and could no longer fly. So I thought, and I thought, and I thought some more. I had a magnificent idea! I could fly to the Great Pasture of Yellow Flowers.

I began my journey and saw my friend Ryan with a scowl on his face. My stomach rumbled, but I knew Ryan needed my help. So I flew as fast as my wings would flap.

Ryan was pulling on his kite. He said, "I wanted to fly my new kite, but the wind blew it to the top of that tree. Now it's stuck."

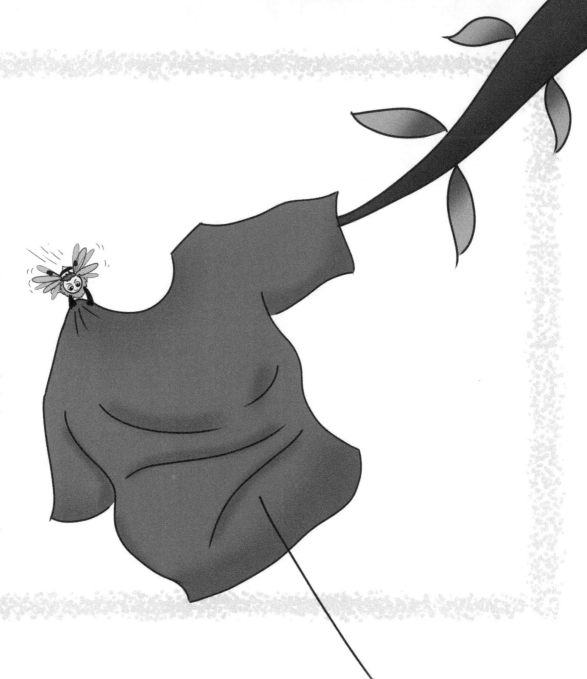

"Silly Ryan," I said. "I can buzz my way to your kite and guide it out of the tree."

I inched the tangled kite out of the branches. *Voilà!*

"Yahoo! Thanks, Brandon the Bee," said Ryan.

I proclaimed, "Bee kind. That's what I do."
I continued to fly toward the Great Pasture of Yellow Flowers.

Then I saw Amy holding her head in her hands. Amy always wore a happy face, but not this time.

"Are you okay?"

"No. My beach ball has floated away, and I don't know how to swim."

"I can help you."

I flew behind the beach ball and pushed it over to Amy.

My stomach roared. Amy laughed and told me that she had a cheeseburger with chili cheese fries and a strawberry milkshake that she could share.

"I can't eat your food. I only eat nectar from my favorite flowers, and I have to get some quickly."

As I zipped on my way, I said, "Bee kind. That's what I do."

I heard whimpering coming from Katie's backyard.

"Katie, why are you crying?"

"I lost Teddy Bear and can't find him."

"Can I help you?"

"Yes, please, but I've looked everywhere."

"Let's look together," I said.

Katie and I looked behind the rocks and near the bushes, but we couldn't find Teddy Bear.

We searched by the swing set and even in the sandbox, but again, no Teddy Bear.

Then I buzzed into the sky, and what did I see behind a tree? Teddy Bear!

Katie screeched with joy. "Yes, yes, yes! Thank you, Brandon the Bee."

At that moment, my stomach growled.

"You must be very hungry. Here's my peanut butter and jelly sandwich topped with lots of cheese and some chocolate ice cream with sprinkles," Katie said.

"Oh, I only eat nectar."

Time was ticking, so I hurried on my way.

My stomach continued to rumble, but I knew I had to bee kind to others along the way. I flew closer and closer and imagined the nectar waiting for me! *Mmmmm.*

I flew so fast that I started spinning out of control tumbling from the tops of the trees. *Splash*!

"Help!"

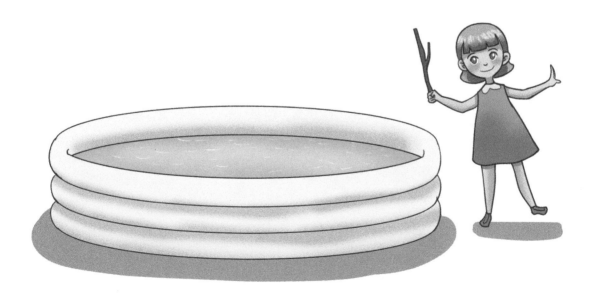

Out of nowhere, a strange-looking creature that was very kind reached into the water and saved me.

When my wings dried, I performed a happy dance, and once again, I was on my way.

And then...wait—yes! The Great Pasture of Yellow Flowers! I was so excited to finally arrive that I stopped flying in mid-air and face-planted into the nectar. I ate and danced and ate some more.

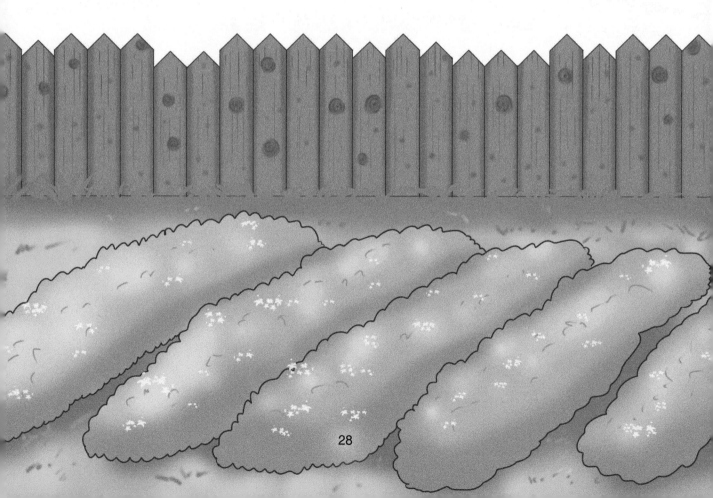

As I sprawled on the grass and looked up at the clouds, I smiled and said, "*Bee kind.* That's what we *all* should do."

About the Author

Jan Sherman is a children's book lover. *Bee Kind* is the first book written in her Brandon the Bee™ series, sharing simple life lessons with children. Jan lives in Phoenix, Arizona, with her husband and two spoiled Yorkies. You can visit her at Be-in-couraged.com.

Be-In-Couraged is an outreach of
MSW Ministries, a 501 (c)(3) organization